COLONEL PARKINSON IN CHARGE

# COLONEL PARKINSON IN CHARGE

## A WRY REFLECTION ON MY INCURABLE ILLNESS

### FRANÇOIS GRAVEL

TRANSLATED BY
SHELLEY POMERANCE

ANANSI

First published as *À vos ordres, colonel Parkinson!* in 2019 by Les Éditions Québec Amérique Inc.
First published in English in 2023 by House of Anansi Press Inc.
houseofanansi.com

House of Anansi Press is committed to protecting our natural environment. This book is made
of material from well-managed FSC®-certified forests, recycled materials, and other
controlled sources.

House of Anansi Press is a Global Certified Accessible™ (GCA by Benetech) publisher.
The ebook version of this book meets stringent accessibility standards and is available to readers
with print disabilities.

27  26  25  24  23    1  2  3  4  5

Library and Archives Canada Cataloguing in Publication

Title: Colonel Parkinson in charge : a wry reflection on my incurable illness / François Gravel ;
translated by Shelley Pomerance.
Other titles: À vos ordres, colonel Parkinson! English
Names: Gravel, François, author. | Pomerance, Shelley, translator.
Identifiers: Canadiana (print) 20220424055 | Canadiana (ebook) 20220424136 |
ISBN 9781487010300 (softcover) | ISBN 9781487010317 (EPUB)
Subjects: LCSH: Gravel, François. | LCSH: Gravel, François—Health. | LCSH: Parkinson's
disease. | LCSH: Parkinson's disease—Patients—Québec (Province)—Biography. | CSH: Authors,
Canadian (French)—Québec (Province)—20th century—Biography. | LCGFT: Autobiographies.
Classification: LCC PS8563.R388 A713 2023 | DDC C843/.54—dc23

Book design: Lucia Kim
Cover image: Brain image by jcomp on Freepik; Star image by Freepik
The typeface used for the chapter titles is Shake, which was created from the real handwriting of
a person living with Parkinson's Disease. Learn more at writewithparkinsons.com.

*House of Anansi Press respectfully acknowledges that the land on which we operate is the Traditional
Territory of many Nations, including the Anishinabeg, the Wendat, and the Haudenosaunee. It is also the
Treaty Lands of the Mississaugas of the Credit.*

 Canada Council
for the Arts
Conseil des Arts
du Canada
 ONTARIO ARTS COUNCIL
CONSEIL DES ARTS DE L'ONTARIO
an Ontario government agency
un organisme du gouvernement de l'Ontario

With the participation of the Government of Canada
Avec la participation du gouvernement du Canada     Canadä

*We acknowledge the financial support of the Government of Canada through the National Translation
Program for Book Publishing, an initiative of the Action Plan for Official Languages—2018–2023:
Investing in Our Future, for our translation activities.*

Printed and bound in Canada

MIX
Paper from
responsible sources
FSC
www.fsc.org    FSC® C103567

# Contents

# Frisbee

I'VE NEVER BEEN GOOD AT sports. It's a matter of coordination, I suppose, or balance, or body type. It's very likely that all of these reasons are valid, along with a few others I'm not even aware of. In high school, when it came time to pick teams, I was always one of the last to be chosen. With good reason, I'm sorry to say. If it had been up to me, I wouldn't have chosen myself.

I hated gym class, though that never prevented me from playing sports with friends on the street. I'm the product of an era when all you had to do was stick your nose outside to find enough kids to form two teams for just about any sport. When

I was with my friends, I could imagine that I was Maurice Richard, Jacques Plante, or Yogi Berra, who had a long career as a baseball catcher before becoming a famous philosopher. I loved this way of playing sports: we could mix up the teams when they were unbalanced, invent our own rules, and play for hours on end without a teacher cutting us down to size. Total bliss.

Inevitably, over time this group of friends disbanded, though I still see my old pal Bernard, with whom I never miss an opportunity to throw anything that's somewhat round and flies through the air. Sixty years later, childhood is not that far behind us.

A few years ago, Bernard and I were up at the cottage, tossing around a Frisbee, when suddenly I noticed something strange: I was unable to throw the Frisbee properly. Even when I concentrated, the Frisbee seemed to systematically land in the hedge or on a neighbour's lawn.

I may not be a great athlete, but I do know how to throw a Frisbee in a straight line. You hold it firmly and let go at just the right time—it's not that complicated. Over the last half-century, I've done it hundreds of times, so why couldn't I do it now? I gave it another spin, straight into the hedge. Maybe I was concentrating too hard or I was too tense. I tried to relax before throwing it again, but no luck: the Frisbee landed on the neighbour's lawn. I got the feeling that Bernard was growing tired of jumping over the fence to rescue the disc, but I tried one last experiment and threw it with my left hand. I succeeded on the very first try, even though I'm usually completely ham-fisted with my left hand.

Eventually, we grew tired of this frustrating back and forth and joined our wives, who were waiting to have a drink on the terrace. I told them what had just happened to me, deciding to make light of it: it's not so serious; most likely it's just a temporary problem; it's part of the pact I've made with old age, this new friend who, in return, has endowed me with wisdom, serenity, emotional intelligence, patience, experience, erudition, and so many other joys that those younger than me aren't even aware of. I can imagine living the rest of my life without tossing any Frisbees at all, if that's the price to pay for all these advantages.

During my friends' stay at the cottage, I made an effort to be an accommodating host, though at times I was a bit distracted: a seed had been sown in my brain, and a nasty plant had begun to sprout there.

* * *

OVER THE NEXT TWO YEARS, I felt myself aging at an accelerated rate. I tired easily and couldn't do without my midday nap. At times, Michèle, my beloved, pointed out that I dragged my feet while walking and my back hunched over. My brother-in-law mentioned that my gait had changed and my right arm was bent, as if I had it in a sling. When I was aware of it, I managed, without too much effort, to persuade my arm to behave normally, but as soon as I got lost in thought—which is, after all, the whole point of going for a walk—I would bend forward unconsciously and my arm would fold up, like a football player guarding the ball while wending his way through enemy lines. I also ran more slowly, and for the last while had been letting Michèle overtake me on our daily jog.

The act of writing also presented some interesting challenges. If my handwriting has always been atrocious, it now became absolutely illegible, even to me. It seemed my right hand no longer obeyed my brain: even if I told it to form large letters, it could produce only an increasingly tiny, spidery scrawl. If a word had more than three syllables, the last syllable would be twice as small as the first, as if the muscles of my hand refused to co-operate. If I lived in a world without computers or typewriters, I would have had to stop writing stories, which would be a lot more stressful for me than giving up my dream of one day becoming a champion at ultimate Frisbee.

The situation became embarrassing when I had to sign books at book fairs. I could manage only a horrible scribble, and I blamed myself: *Children deserve something better, François. No one is asking you to turn yourself into a monk who copies dainty illuminations, but to write legibly is not all that difficult. Make an effort...*

But even when I applied myself, all I could manage was a clumsy smudge. I tried to make excuses by laying the blame on computers—these days, who still writes by hand?—but I found myself less and less credible.

I began to suspect that I was afflicted with something other than simple old age, but what?

* * *

IT WASN'T UNTIL TWO YEARS after the Frisbee incident that I thought of mentioning my little problems to my family physician, though it wouldn't have taken much to let another year go by before broaching the topic. He was still busily renewing my regular prescription for statins, at the end of the consultation, when I finally brought up the Frisbee, my posture, my new habit of carrying my right arm as if it was in a sling...

Cholesterol was suddenly the last of his worries. He tapped a few words on his keyboard. Judging by his frown, what he saw in response didn't appear to be very reassuring.

"Have you had a concussion recently?" he asked me.

"No..."

"Or a fall?"

"No..."

I got the feeling my answers weren't satisfactory, but he went on with his interrogation.

"Do you ever feel unsteady on your feet?"

"When I stand up too quickly, yes, I feel dizzy..."

At that he showed more interest, as if he'd hit

upon a promising lead. I wished he would tilt his screen toward me, but soon there was no need for that.

"Do you have a tremor?"

"No..."

"Are you sure?"

"It seems to me that I would be aware of it..."

"It would be best if I sent you to a neurologist. But don't hesitate to come back and see me. It may not be anything major, but I'm curious to know what the diagnosis is."

The word *Parkinson's* was never uttered during this conversation, but then and there, it started flashing in my brain. And it would never switch off.

\* \* \*

WHEN I GOT HOME, I DID WHAT anyone would do under the circumstances: I turned on my laptop and googled *Parkinson's*.

The first thing I read was that it's important to think of this word as a plural; not everyone has the same symptoms—there isn't *one* Parkinson's but rather *several* Parkinson's. For example, some people with Parkinson's don't have a tremor. Which didn't exactly reassure me.

I went through the list of symptoms, each more appealing than the last: a slow, shuffling walk; a tendency to take small steps; a reduction in facial expression, fine motor dexterity, and sense of smell; an increase in sweating and urinary frequency; smaller handwriting, also known as micrographia; falls, constipation, excess saliva, dizziness, a burning sensation, impatience, fatigue, hallucinations, depression, dementia...To complete the picture, all that was missing were the bubonic plague, syphilis, and gangrene, but I was sure they would turn up if I kept surfing the web.

While the symptoms of Parkinson's vary, the definition is always the same, and it's awful: a *degenerative* neurological disease. If I didn't have a tremor yet, I just had to wait around, and God only knew what I would degenerate into next.

The websites I consulted didn't miss an opportunity to remind me that I shouldn't count on a cure: no one knows what causes this illness, for which there is no remedy. And only a few symptoms can be relieved.

I closed my laptop. I no longer needed a doctor

to confirm that I had the illness, even though I found it hard to believe. As the saying goes, I felt as if a ton of bricks had fallen on my head. But I managed to go and find Michèle to tell her what I'd just learned.

"Everyone turns into a hypochondriac when they surf the internet," she said to reassure me. "At least wait to see a neurologist before jumping to any conclusions."

She changed her mind, however, when she read the list of symptoms: the only one missing was "difficulty throwing a Frisbee."

Let's face facts, Michèle: those really are bricks that have fallen on my head. Just take a look— there's a whole pile of them around me.

* * *

WHEN I MANAGED TO GET AN appointment with a specialist, I told my story yet again, from the Frisbee to my chicken-scratch handwriting. I saw him nodding and imagined him ticking boxes in his head: *check, check, check.*

That day, I learned that a diagnosis for Parkinson's disease is not made by a blood test,

X-ray, or some sort of puncture. Rather, in the absence of a biological marker, the neurologist relies on the patient's description of his symptoms and on his own observations.

"Have you noticed any decrease in your sense of taste or smell?"

"Yes, a little, but they were never particularly well developed."

"Has anyone in your family had Parkinson's?"

"My mother was diagnosed with it when she was ninety-five. It's kind of normal at that age, isn't it? It would have been a miracle if she hadn't had any illness."

He agreed, then asked me to step into the examining room, where he proceeded to give me a series of tests: walk, watch his fingers, move my eyes, wrists, touch my nose with my index finger. (I enjoyed this last test, which I passed without any difficulty.)

In his autobiography *Lucky Man: A Memoir*, the actor Michael J. Fox writes about consulting one of the most famous American neurologists when he thought he might have Parkinson's disease. Among other things, this eminent specialist asked him to touch the tip of his nose with his finger.

If, in another life, I become a doctor, I will choose neurology over urology—their tests are much less intrusive.

My diagnosis (I was about to write *verdict*) didn't take long: "You do indeed have Parkinson's disease," the neurologist told me. "For now, it's mild..."

"But it's going to get worse..."

He nodded and went on, very slowly. He probably suspected that I was shaken by this revelation. I figured he'd seen the whole gamut of reactions when he delivered this news, and that it wasn't his favourite part of the job.

"It's too early to prescribe any medication," he said. "Come back to see me in six months. We'll see how the illness develops."

*     *     *

IT WOULD BE AN OVERSTATEMENT to claim that the diagnosis was good news, but at least it set the record straight. In a sense, I felt relieved. Once something bad has been identified, you have a better idea of how to deal with it. I was neither the first nor the only person to have this illness, there were lots of resources available, and I was in good hands. Things weren't so bad.

What you tell yourself rationally is one thing; whether you choose to believe it is something else. That would be too easy. The bricks didn't fall quite so hard over the next few days, but they did keep falling. Even though I knew I should use them to build myself a new house, I hadn't found the architect's drawings. And while I was waiting to find them, I felt like I was going in circles and getting nowhere.

I didn't give a hoot if I shook a bit, ran more slowly, or lost my sense of taste. But dementia? What if my grandchildren had a grandfather who was gaga? *Why does Grandpa shake all the time?* What if Michèle was condemned to becoming a caregiver? *Open the garage door, yummy, yummy, here comes some tasty purée, be careful not to choke on it...*

Over the next six months, during which my main occupation was brooding, these thoughts were the ones that pained me the most. I had plans for my old age, and Parkinson's wasn't one of them.

*  *  *

I'VE OFTEN READ IN BOOKS and articles on
psychology that a person's frame of mind is, to a
great extent, innate. Some people are born happy
and will endure the worst hardship with a smile
on their face. Others come into the world down-
cast and remain that way for the rest of their lives.

Obviously, your frame of mind will vary
depending on what happens to you, but it will
always go back to its point of departure. Lottery
winners will be happier than usual for six months,
but the needle will return to its regular place on
the dial. On the other hand, someone who has
had a limb amputated will see their mood descend
below average for six months before it rises again.

I don't know whether I believe this theory, but
I waited more than a year before starting to write
this book. Now I am ready to build something
with the bricks that fell on my head. Each of us has
our own way of coping with hardship. Mine is to
sit down in front of my computer and tell stories.

## James Parkinson

THE TERRIBLE PARALYSIS THAT STEPHEN Hawking, the famous astrophysicist, suffered from is amyotrophic lateral sclerosis, or ALS. The Americans call it Lou Gehrig's disease, after a baseball player who had the illness. It's not often that a disease is named after a patient who suffered from it. Disease is a physician's business. In Europe, they call ALS Charcot's disease in memory of the famous French neurologist.

Alois Alzheimer, Hans Asperger, Georges Gilles de la Tourette, Jean-Martin Charcot, and James Parkinson were all physicians. Each made major discoveries, but wasn't there a better way to honour their work than naming illnesses after them? Did anyone stop to think that these learned men might have children who would be ridiculed in the schoolyard and might not want to spend their adult years explaining their surname? And what about declarations made in church or at city hall? "Juliet Alzheimer-Parkinson, do you take Romeo Asperger-Tourette to be your lawfully wedded husband?"

One thing is certain: James Parkinson never asked for his patronymic to become a household name, a process the linguists call antonomasia.

This English doctor, born in 1755, was a fascinating character. In addition to his work as a physician, Parkinson was known for his social and political engagement, much like Norman Bethune. He sat in the House of Commons, where he was an ardent defender of the disadvantaged, fighting in particular for increasingly progressive taxation and more humane conditions in the "insane asylums." A partisan during the French Revolution, he is said to have plotted to assassinate George III. This scheme, called the Popgun Plot, involved using a poison dart fired from a gun. Needless to say, the attempt failed;

otherwise, the word *Parkinson* would now be associated with regicide instead of disease. Parkinson was called before the Privy Council, where he refused to testify under oath for fear of incriminating himself. Fortunately for him, the affair had no repercussions.

His inquiring mind then turned to geology and paleontology, new sciences that, at the time, inspired passionate interest among scholars and amateurs alike. His collection of ancient stones and fossils was renowned throughout Europe. I also read that he encouraged all medical doctors to use stenography, a method he himself used to write his patients' files, as well as his scientific articles and books. I suspect that a number of his colleagues misunderstood his message and felt obligated to *always* use stenography, even when writing out prescriptions.

We know Parkinson's name today thanks to a short text he published in 1817. *An Essay on the Shaking Palsy.* Another way of putting it might be "trembling paralysis," which is a lovely oxymoron. He described the illness as follows: "Involuntary tremulous motion, with lessened muscular power, in parts not in action and even when supported;

with a propensity to bend the trunk forwards, and to pass from a walking to a running pace: the senses and intellects being uninjured."

These symptoms had all been known for a long time. You can find references to them on Egyptian papyrus dating from the twelfth century BCE, and numerous passages in the Bible mention tremors. It's quite possible that King David suffered from them. In his essay, Parkinson quoted Galen, the brilliant physician from Greek antiquity, who described tremors that occurred while at rest, postural problems, and paralysis. However, it was Parkinson who connected all of these symptoms and came up with a description that is still relevant today—with one omission: one in three people living with Parkinson's will suffer from dementia. (In conducting my research, I read that people who have Parkinson's are six times more likely to suffer from dementia than those who don't have the disease. Even though I know the two statistics are mathematically compatible, I prefer the first one. Better yet, I like to think that those with Parkinson's have a two-out-of-three chance of *not* having dementia. Some statistics are worth more than any number of pills.)

Surprisingly, to arrive at this conclusion, Parkinson examined just six patients: the first three in his office and two others in the street. As for the sixth, he observed him only from a distance. Certain sources go so far as to claim that he gave only one of them a physical exam.

When you think about it, it's not all that strange. The gait of individuals who have Parkinson's is so typical that I recognize it easily, and I'm no doctor. This can be illustrated by showing the famous and oft-repeated caricature of the progression of humanity from the Stone Age to the Information Age: a hairy and stooped prehistoric man straightens up as he evolves, before ending up bent over a computer in a position that is an exact replica of the first. Leaning forward, a person with Parkinson's is often off balance, which explains the small steps that make them "pass from a walking to a running pace," as Parkinson described it, and can, unfortunately, cause them to fall.

James Parkinson's essay doesn't seem to have captured his contemporaries' interest, since he died in relative anonymity. It was another several decades before he was rediscovered by Jean-Martin Charcot.

If Parkinson was a remarkable man, Charcot was a medical giant. In addition to heading a department at Paris's Salpêtrière, at the time one of the world's largest hospices, with over ten thousand patients, he published countless articles on mental illness. Among other things, he believed that hysteria was a bona fide illness, and not something feigned, and that it wasn't exclusive to women, which caused a real uproar among his colleagues. (It would be another century before this word, derived from the Latin *hystericus*, which means "related to the uterus," would be replaced by *histrionic personality disorder*.)

Charcot's observations of his patients also allowed him to discover that, contrary to popular belief at the time, the shaking palsy and multiple sclerosis were two distinct illnesses. In addition, he conducted a number of experiments on hypnosis. Freud was Charcot's student before becoming one of his first translators into German.

Unlike Parkinson, Charcot did not go unrecognized during his lifetime. In 1881, three thousand representatives from around the world paid tribute to him during an international medical congress in London, England. During a ceremony that also celebrated his compatriot Louis Pasteur, he saw his face portrayed in a fireworks display. These days, scientists rarely get this kind of reception, the red-carpet treatment being reserved instead for reality TV stars.

In 1884, Charcot became a leading socialite, playing host to Edmond de Goncourt, Alphonse Daudet, Émile Zola, Anatole France, Guy de Maupassant, and Jules Renard—in other words, all the writers, which in France amounted to everyone who was considered important.

Charcot was impressed by Parkinson's essay, which he became aware of in 1864. In *Leçons du Mardi à la Salpêtrière, 1887–1888* (as translated by Stewart A. Factor and William J. Weiner in *Parkinson's Disease: Diagnosis and Clinical Management*), Charcot advised his students to "read the entire book and it will provide you with the satisfaction and knowledge that one always gleans from a direct clinical description made by an honest and careful observer." It was Charcot who was the first to associate *disease* and *Parkinson*, which was, all in all, an excellent idea: it's unlikely that James Parkinson was celebrated with fireworks during his lifetime, but he deserves our recognition; plus, if you consider that Galen called this disease *cato-che*, from the Greek verb meaning "to withhold, to seize," you realize what a close call we had. Parkinson's sounds so much better, doesn't it?

\* \* \*

IF YOU SURF THE INTERNET looking for information about James Parkinson, as I just did, you will come upon a photograph of a young man with an intelligent look, endowed with wide sideburns, a full beard, and an elegant moustache. You wouldn't doubt for an instant that he was a great scientist from the nineteenth century. He suits the part perfectly. There's just one bothersome detail: all the iterations of the photograph are identical, except that in some he's looking to the left and in others, to the right.

The mystery deepens when you consider that photography was invented in 1826 and James Parkinson died two years earlier, in 1824, at the age of sixty-nine. And the man who appears in the photograph is clearly much younger.

Several authors have mentioned this incongruity, and all of the serious websites state that no portrait of our doctor exists. It seems our James has been confused with a certain James Cumine Parkinson, an Irishman born in 1832. His father intended for him to become a doctor, but since his grades in the classics were insufficient, he had to pursue another career. He enlisted in the navy, tried his luck prospecting for gold in Australia, and wound up in Tasmania.

So the photograph is the portrait of a man who is not who we think he is, and who found a unique way to go down in history.

Subject erroneously identified as Dr. James Parkinson. Since the earliest photograph of a person dates from 1839, it is impossible for this to be the real Dr. James Parkinson, who died in 1824.

As a certain J. G. Rowntree once said, referring to the other Parkinson—the real one, if I may put it that way—"English born, English bred, forgotten by the English and the world at large, such was the fate of James Parkinson."

*  *  *

I LIKE THE IDEA THAT the main character in our story is faceless: we can depict him as we wish.

My personal Parkinson has a moustache, beard, and sideburns, as in the photograph, but I have assigned him the rank of colonel in an imaginary army and have dressed him in a uniform befitting his title, with an abundance of medals and gold braid, not to mention protuberant epaulettes on his shoulders. When I don't feel up to my morning jog, I hear him shouting so loudly that I'm obliged to obey. I no longer have any choice in the matter: he's already in charge.

# Vocabulary

I'VE OFTEN TRIED TO EXPLAIN my new condition to family and friends, but I'm unable to find satisfactory wording. While you can have a tumour or a cold, you can't "have a Parkinson's."

And if I say I have Parkinson's disease, it sounds overly dramatic. While I am, in fact, plagued by all kinds of stiffness and I feel weak, as if an intruder twenty years older than me has taken control of my muscles, I don't really experience physical pain, at least not at this phase of the illness. A toothache is much more painful. The more I think about it, the more it strikes me that the most appropriate way to put it is a bad pun: since my diagnosis, I've been feeling Parkinstunned.

# Lawn Bowling

SO I WOULDN'T HAVE TO REPEAT the same information ten times over, and to avoid making people feel uncomfortable, a few hours after receiving my diagnosis I sent those closest to me an email with the heading "Health Report":

Some of you already know, while others don't. As I don't want to have to repeat the following, I thought it made sense to send this group email to give you the rotten news. I've just been to see the neurologist, who confirmed what I've suspected for a while: I have Parkinson's disease. As you may already know, this disease is degenerative (how

I love that word!) and incurable, though certain medications can relieve the symptoms.

The good news is that I'm not there yet. The doctor believes that I'm in the early stages of the disease and wants to see how it progresses before prescribing any medication. For now, he recommends that I stay in shape, remain as active as possible, and drink a glass of wine every evening (I would have preferred that he prescribe ice cream, but I'm willing to comply). It's impossible to predict how quickly the illness will progress. I hope it won't be in too much of a hurry.

For the time being, I don't have the tremors that are typical of the disease (those of you who are older might remember Diefenbaker), but my balance is affected, my gait is odd (let's say, odder than it usually is!), and my right hand has a tendency to go on strike.

All of this prevents me from indulging in some of my favourite activities (line dancing, lawn bowling, and playing cup-and-ball), though fortunately, it doesn't prevent me from writing, reading, walking, running, gazing at the river, listening to music, or losing at Scrabble. Come to think of it, it makes these activities even more enjoyable.

IT'S NOW TWO YEARS LATER, and I wouldn't change a word of this email, though I have since learned that John Diefenbaker suffered not from Parkinson's disease but from "essential tremor." More on that later.

# Reactions

YOU KNOW YOU HAVE AN incurable degenerative disease when the people you tell the news to
barely manage to refrain from wishing you a speedy
recovery. You'll have to admit that you've put their
tactfulness to the test. If, under the circumstances,
showing that they're devastated displays a lack of
tact ("My God, how terrible! How much time before
you develop dementia?"), trying to minimize the
problem is just as bad ("It's just a rough patch;
you'll get over it! Did I tell you I have two cavities
that need to be filled? These things only happen
to me!"). Some people ask questions, others don't.
Nothing could be more normal. How would they

know whether you feel like sharing your worries or if you'd like something to take your mind off things?

A distant acquaintance might, to your great surprise, show compassion that comes across as appropriate and sincere, while old friends appear to be unmoved. Don't be fooled: some people might be as stunned as you are and not want to show it, while others will take more time to absorb the news.

Some will suggest that you stuff yourself with turmeric, or deprive yourself of any food whose name begins with two consonants, or move your bed so that it captures certain energies. I strongly advise against engaging in a discussion with them on the fundamentals of the scientific method. Tell yourself they have the best of intentions, which is basically true. If they persist, you can always reply that your neurologist appears to be competent and has proved it by asking you to touch the tip of your nose, an activity at which you have become expert. You can even demonstrate it for them. They'll be impressed.

# The Black Substance

OUR KNOWLEDGE OF THIS DISEASE has, of course, advanced greatly since James Parkinson penned his essay, but the exact causes are still unknown. We are indebted to a certain Konstantin Tretiakoff, who discovered that the principal cerebral structure affected is the substantia nigra, a finding only widely accepted in 1938. It wasn't until 1950 that the role played by dopamine was understood, thanks to the efforts of Arvid Carlsson, a Swedish physician.

But perhaps you don't feel like reading a long list of doctors' names. Nor is it likely that you're familiar with monoamine oxidase B or catechol-O-methyltransferase inhibitors. Good thing: me neither. I'm not very credible when it comes to medicine, since I remember nothing from my high school biology course, except for the beef heart we dissected and subsequently left to rot in a classmate's desk during the Christmas vacation. When we returned to class in January, we had to keep the windows open for a whole week—in winter. Fifty years later, I still get a whiff of rotting meat when I walk past my old school.

My undeniable incompetence in medicine won't prevent me from explaining to you what I've retained from my reading and my own experience. Parkinson's begins with the loss of cells in a part of the brain stem known as the substantia nigra (Latin for "black substance," a great title for a Stephen King novel, don't you think?) due to its particular pigmentation (as you might have guessed). I'd like to point out that this zone is tiny, and the grey matter so dear to Hercule Poirot is not affected.

No one knows exactly why the cells of the black substance die before any others. Pesticides are often blamed—some convincing studies seem to demonstrate that Parkinson's disease has more victims in agricultural zones—but that would explain only a higher incidence of the disease, not its principal cause; very few pesticides were in use during Galen's lifetime.

By the time a neurologist makes a diagnosis, it's estimated that 80 percent of the substantia nigra's cells have already ceased functioning. When a patient goes for a consultation because they have trouble throwing a Frisbee, it's already too late. The cells have died and can never be resuscitated. But even if the patient had discovered the issue earlier, it wouldn't have changed things, since there is no known cure.

The cells of the black substance are responsible for the production of dopamine, a chemical element that plays a number of roles, some of them surprising. Dopamine allows certain insects to develop an exoskeleton and mussels to have exceptional adhesive properties, for example, which is always good to know.

In humans, dopamine acts, among other things, as a messenger among the brain cells involved in muscle control and fluidity of movement, which explains why it's called a neurotransmitter. When the dopamine factory goes on strike, its production is ensured by a reduced staff that is clearly less effective, or perhaps is overworked. The remaining dopamine starts to give strange orders to certain muscles (to shake, for example), or gives no orders at all, and the patient becomes temporarily paralyzed.

There are over 600 muscles in the body, 639 to be precise. Obviously, the role they play in movement is essential—which explains the characteristic gait and slowness of those who have Parkinson's—not to mention their role in digestion, swallowing, producing sound, speaking, writing, and throwing a Frisbee. Muscles also control facial expression, so those affected by this disease may at times appear to be expressionless due to a lack of adequate muscular activity.

As a neurotransmitter, dopamine acts more precisely as a movement *trigger*. When you set out for a walk, the first step is often difficult, as the brain has to function without dopamine when first commanding the legs to walk. Once they've understood what they need to do, the legs manage rather well, at least until they encounter an unexpected obstacle. Then you have to start all over again. The brain has to consciously give a command for almost every movement.

Dopamine plays several other roles. For example, it's released during pleasant experiences, such as when taking drugs. As a result, it plays a part in addiction, but it's also linked to feelings of love and sexual pleasure. In addition, it reinforces actions that are usually beneficial, such as eating healthy foods and exercising, and acts as a reward system. Individuals who have too much dopamine tend to suffer from schizophrenia, while those who don't have enough often become depressed. Rare is the person with Parkinson's who escapes the latter. I'm no exception. Fortunately, I have some experience in this area.

\* \* \*

THE GLOBAL ECONOMY EXPERIENCED ITS Great Depression during the last century, in the 1930s. Since I was born in 1951, I have an ironclad alibi: I had nothing to do with it. On a rather different scale, I had an equally severe depression in 1996. At that time, I produced a large amount of black substance, but unfortunately it wasn't the same kind I'm lacking now. Rather, I had become a factory for the production of dark thoughts. I felt sad the moment I got out of bed, it continued all day, and it got worse in the evening. It felt like the lenses in my glasses had been tampered with, allowing me to see only my faults and amplifying them. All the mistakes I had made in my life, all the stupid things I'd done or said, all my little acts of cowardice came to mind and struck me as unpardonable crimes. The judge who had installed himself in my brain was implacable, making no allowances for mitigating circumstances.

Permanent sadness, fatigue, lack of energy, difficulty concentrating, I had it all, with the exception, perhaps, of suicidal thoughts, though if the situation had gone on a little longer, just a few months more...

As depression was a fairly common experience in my family, I knew how to deal with it: my doctor prescribed antidepressants, and I saw a psychologist, who helped me lighten the load. I also began seriously training to run, which did me a lot of good. When my doctor found out, he reduced my dose of antidepressants. The message did not fall on deaf ears.

※ ※ ※

WHEN MY NEUROLOGIST TOLD ME I had Parkinson's disease, I may have uttered an emphatic "*Shit*," but I don't recall feeling particularly angry. Kicking one of the four pillars that hold up the heavens would have been justifiable, but I couldn't find them.

When they get news of this kind, many patients feel guilty: *What could I have done to prevent this?* Since I don't see what I could have changed in my lifestyle, the idea never even crossed my mind. Drowning my despair in alcohol didn't occur to me either; that would simply have given me one more problem to deal with. I didn't even protest that it wasn't fair. Why is this happening to me? Because it is, that's all.

On the other hand, the symptoms of depression descended on me, brick by brick: sadness, fatigue, lack of energy, difficulty concentrating...

Having been through it before, I recognized it easily and relied on the same solutions: first, a small dose of antidepressants—please, doctor, it would be stupid to deprive myself. Then I visited my psychologist a few times, but we quickly came to the conclusion that this depression was more chemical than psychological. I didn't need to change my glasses or fire the judge who'd taken up residence in my brain. I'd already done that. Rather than tell the psychologist, yet again, about my childhood, I chose to buy myself a new pair of running shoes. Parkinson's might make me drag my feet, but I would drag them as quickly as possible.

# I'm Writing to You with My Left Hand

I'VE ALWAYS BEEN FASCINATED BY the speed at which young children learn to speak. At one year old, they babble a few sounds, and we get all choked up when, quite by chance, they utter a "mama" or a "dada." A few months later, they've acquired a vocabulary of about a hundred words and manage to make themselves understood. At four years old, they understand the meaning of over two thousand words. They can conjugate verbs and form complex sentences. Of course, it will take them a while to pronounce the more difficult sounds, such as *th* and *r*, and even longer to master the rule for irregular verbs in the past tense, if they ever do, but the basic work is done. Personally, I'd be very happy if I could speak Mandarin as well as a four-year-old Chinese child, even if I had to be corrected when I said the Mandarin equivalent of "they goed." If I spent the rest of my life studying that language, I might succeed, but I would always have an identifiable accent—to the extent, obviously, that the Chinese recognize my Québécois accent.

What has struck me since I joined the Parkinson's clan is that it takes much more time for children to master skills that, to adults, seem so simple, such as snapping your fingers, tying your shoelaces, or whistling. Now that my right hand is partly out of order, I have a better understanding of the degree to which certain actions that become automatic responses for most of us are actually quite complex.

I can still carry a bag or scratch my forehead without having to think about it too much, but not a day goes by that I don't encounter new challenges. Most can be easily circumvented, but I can't take anything for granted. Hundreds of movements that I used to do automatically must now receive conscious commands from my brain, which is forced to find new circuits in order to execute them. I often have the impression that I've unlearned everything I knew—or rather, *everything my right hand knew*—and have to relearn it. Perhaps that's the source of the overwhelming fatigue that affects people with Parkinson's and never lets up.

The best example of these difficulties I can provide is the everyday act of brushing my teeth. Picking up the brush, putting toothpaste on it, and bringing it up to my mouth doesn't present a particular problem, though these actions do require an unusual level of concentration. It's the next step that gets complicated. The up-and-down movement that one does so mechanically it's become an automatic response is blocked: the toothbrush stays there, frozen, as my right hand waits for a command from my brain that never comes. No matter how patient I am, this mechanism that once seemed so natural will never be reactivated. In fact, it would be easier to hold the toothbrush in place and move my head, which would be rather ridiculous.

Fortunately, a few solutions are available to the tooth brusher with Parkinson's disease who is in search of oral hygiene. For example, you can activate certain areas of the brain and order the hand to execute, one by one, each movement required for a good brushing: "Up, down, up, down," and so on for each tooth. It may work, but there are other ways I'd rather spend my days.

Now for the second solution. When nothing goes right, go left. That is, use your left hand. You might get better at it with a bit of practice, but no matter what you do, that hand will always be a bit gauche. Unless of course, you're a lefty. In any case, it's very likely that eventually you will also develop rigidity in that hand.

Fortunately, there's a third solution—a miraculous one: the electric toothbrush.

According to Wikipedia, this marvel of modern technology was invented in 1954 by Dr. Philippe-Guy Woog. It's a great injustice that his name doesn't appear on the list of Nobel laureates. At the very least, they could have named this indispensable object after him: "Michèle, have you seen my woog?" It sounds good to me, and could be quite useful in Scrabble.

Now, if a brilliant engineer would only take on the problem of dental floss, it would be much appreciated.

Let's stay in the bathroom for another moment or two. Imagine having only one good hand to cut your fingernails, pluck your eyebrows, or tap lightly on a bottle of pills to extract just one tablet (don't bother trying it).

Putting on a sweater can quickly become a source of frustration, and taking it off is even worse, especially if it's polar fleece, in which case it seems to be made entirely of Velcro. Now imagine lacing your shoes, tightening a belt, lining up the two sections of a zipper, putting on gloves, buttoning a shirt...By the way, did you know that priests' cassocks were fastened with thirty-three buttons, a figure that represents the number of years Christ spent on earth? (We seem to have lost count of the years he's spent in heaven.) Given the average age of priests and the probability that they suffer from Parkinson's, I understand why they traded in this garment for secular wear.

I imagine it would be difficult to knot a tie neatly, but I haven't put it to the test yet. That would at least give me a reasonable excuse for screwing it up.

Removing my wallet from my back pocket is another manoeuvre that can be tricky. Taking bills out of it, slipping change into it, and putting the wallet back in its place are equally challenging, all of which can really test a shopkeeper's patience. Add stress to the mix and the experience becomes even more unpleasant.

Let's say I want to go out to a restaurant. Really? Even if I've lost my sense of taste? Strange idea. I know I'll doubtless be offered a bowl of soup (thanks, but I'd rather have a glass of vegetable juice), and my spouse will have to cut my steak. Why not order tofu instead? Since I'm not going to taste anything anyway, I might as well eat something healthy. The fun of twirling spaghetti around my fork is no more than a vague memory; instead, I'll use a spoon—not to help me twirl the pasta but to carry it up to my mouth.

What if I prefer to eat a home-cooked meal. Then I'll have to grate cheese, slice bread, peel carrots, crack and beat eggs...If I plan to eat at a reasonable hour, I'd better leave some of these tasks to my partner, which will allow me to bene-fit from her company. All is not lost. While she cuts the carrots into matchsticks, I'll manipulate the corkscrew without too much difficulty, using my left hand to pour the wine. I'd better use two

hands to bring the glass to my lips, though—
one can never be too careful. Plus, I don't want
to waste this precious medicine, with its twelve
thousand elements that can slow the progress of
the disease. At least that's what my doctor told me,
and I have no reason to doubt his word.

Since, like everyone, I write using a computer,
I've noticed that I have a distinct preference for
the qwerty over the yuiop side of the keyboard and
that my left hand will often come to the rescue of
the right when typing an *m* or a *k*, or to double-
click (damn the inventor of the double-click).

I've had to relearn how to place the letters on
a tile rack when playing Scrabble, fill forms out
by hand, put a key in a lock, go down a staircase,
buckle a seatbelt, dial a phone number on a cell-
phone, write an address on an envelope...

But believe it or not, there are advantages to
relearning all these little movements. Rather than
rambling on like most of my sexagenarian friends,
I make new discoveries every day: *Hmm, putting a
plug in a socket is more complicated than I thought.*
Since there is an infinite number of situations of
this kind, I'll always have something to keep me
busy.

Looking on the bright side of things, I've noticed that I don't have to make an effort to eat more slowly, something recommended by all nutritionists. I also won't need to attend talks by Zen masters to learn to live in the present moment and take one day at a time (in any case, have they ever arrived in packages of ten?). The simplest movement requires all of my concentration, and it's become increasingly difficult to do two things at the same time.

Finally, one skill I still have is that of being able to scratch my right ear. All I need to do is put my pinky finger in my ear for it to start scratching on its own, without my even having to ask! I get the feeling I'm going to make some folks pretty jealous.

# Horseshoe and Rabbit's Foot

IMAGINE, JUST FOR A MOMENT, that illnesses are caused by tiny demons, and that Satan gives each one the order to do as much damage as possible. My own personal demon—let's call him Parky— would get barely a passing grade, if that.

In fact, he could have gone after a young man or woman, which unfortunately happens all too often (incidentally, the disease affects men and women equally, and is not the slightest bit racist). Learning at thirty years of age that you have a degenerative disease must be the equivalent of having a load of steel beams fall on your head instead of a ton of bricks. It would disrupt your career path, to say the least. And what if you happened to be a single mother?

In some cases, Parkinson's is, unfortunately, a passport to unemployment, poverty, social exclusion, and solitude. When you receive this diagnosis at age sixty-five and have a decent pension, you can always tell yourself that from now on that's the label your old age will bear. And if you're lucky enough to have married well, you'll even be able to continue buying bread that isn't presliced.

Think for a moment of all the jobs and hobbies Parkinson's makes more difficult, if not downright impossible: playing a musical instrument, dancing, performing delicate surgical operations or other kinds of needlework, repairing old clocks, filling teeth, styling hair, polishing nails, modelling for an artist ("Sit still, please!"), painting, applying makeup, trying your hand (or feet, rather) at tightrope walking, performing magic, cooking, creating perfumes...

A demon would have to be pretty short on imagination to pick on a guy whose principal pastime is writing novels, an activity for which he needs just two not particularly agile fingers. If those two fingers happen to go on strike, he still has eight others, and if the disease progresses to the point of preventing him from typing, he can always turn to Siri for help.

So what if I'm typing more slowly now? Who cares? It just gives me more time to reflect while writing, a habit I should have acquired decades ago.

I don't know what you were thinking when you chose me, Parky, but you really blew it.

Even worse, you provided me with a subject for a new book. I don't know what your boss will think of what you've done, but you made a real rookie's mistake. You might as well give a country singer a broken heart: he'll simply take advantage of it to write new songs and will end up thanking you.

If Satan ever gives you a new assignment, talk it over with me first, pal: I have a long list of names to suggest.

# Good Grief!

WHEN YOU VISIT INTERNET PAGES such as "Twelve Celebrities Who've Had Parkinson's Disease," you inevitably come across Charles Schulz, the famous creator of good ol' Charlie Brown and his friends Lucy and Linus Van Pelt, Schroeder, and the Little Red-Haired Girl, not to mention Snoopy, my writer colleague.

Schulz struggled with depression his entire life, which didn't prevent him from working tirelessly to supply his readers with their daily dose of drawings. He was a man of few words, and very private, but in the 1980s, he began to complain that his hand shook so much he had to

hold his wrist to sketch his characters. His drawing was increasingly affected by the tremors, as
many readers have observed, but he continued to
write and draw the comic strip until he was diagnosed with cancer and underwent triple bypass
surgery. Struck down by illness, he announced his
retirement in December 1999, at seventy-seven
years of age. At the time, his daily comic strip was
published in twenty-six languages in twenty-six
hundred newspapers worldwide—not bad for a
man who'd always felt rejected. "I simply could
no longer hold the pen," he told a reporter for the
*New York Times*. "Am I supposed to sit here for the
rest of my life, drawing these things while all my
friends die or retire?"

In an interview with Al Roker on *The Today Show*,
Schultz expressed his dismay at the realization he'd
come to, while signing his final strip, that he'd done
wrong by Charlie Brown: "All of a sudden, I thought,
'You know, that poor kid—he never even got to kick
the football.'"

Schulz died two months later. Like Hergé, the
creator of Tintin, he didn't want anyone to replace
him. A wise decision.

However, in surfing the web, I learned that the

problems with Schultz's hand were not caused by Parkinson's disease, as many people thought, but by essential tremor. Unlike the tremors caused by Parkinson's, which occur when you're at rest, essential tremors occur when you're doing an activity. Like drawing, for example. Poor Charles.

So Schulz didn't have Parkinson's, which is too bad: I would gladly have recruited him for the team I'm planning to put together when I get to heaven, even if we'd lose 122 to 0 at baseball and have to fight off kite-eating trees.

\* \* \*

LIKE SCHULZ, JOHNNY CASH, THE man in black, often sided with the dispossessed, whether they were prisoners, alcoholics, loners, poor people, Native Americans, or all of the above. In 1997, struggling with tremors, he cut back on touring, though that didn't prevent him from recording two superb albums, *Solitary Man* and *The Man Comes Around*, on which you can hear him singing in a voice that is hesitant at times, yet always moving.

It seems, however, that contrary to widespread

belief, Cash didn't have Parkinson's either, but rather a similar neurodegenerative disorder. Pneumonia, diabetes, and the profound grief he experienced over the loss of his wife, June Carter, have also been mentioned as possible causes of his death. I'm inclined to attribute it to alcohol and the large quantity and variety of pills that he gobbled as if they were Smarties. Whatever the case may be, I won't be able to recruit him for my team, and I deeply regret it.

*  *  *

WHAT ABOUT MUHAMMAD ALI, FORMERLY Cassius Clay, the boxer well known to crossword puzzle enthusiasts? Didn't he suffer from Parkinson's disease, with a good dose of dementia to boot?

"God gave me Parkinson's disease to show me I'm just a man, just like everybody else," said he who modestly called himself "The Greatest."

Muhammad Ali was indeed a man "like everybody else," though one who fought sixty-one professional heavyweight bouts, each time against opponents who weighed just as much as he did and whose goal was to give him a concussion. During his training sessions, he would lower his guard and ask his partners to hit him in the head to show that he was the strongest. It's been calculated that during his career, he would have received twenty-nine thousand blows to the head. Yet he died at seventy-four years of age. That's rather encouraging, wouldn't you say?

When asked if boxing played a part in his illness, Ali replied, "It wasn't the boxing, it was the autographs!" I understand: it must be difficult signing your name with gloves on.

I haven't acquired a degree in medicine since I started writing this book, but you'll forgive me for doubting whether Muhammad Ali had Parkinson's. Indeed, some doctors have spoken of boxer's dementia, which strikes me as much more likely.

✻ ✻ ✻

LATER, I'LL EXAMINE THE CASES of a few celebrities, dead or alive, who were diagnosed with Parkinson's. One, obviously, is Michael J. Fox, who has been very vocal about it, but there's also Robin Williams, Salvador Dalí, Mao Zedong, Linda Ronstadt, Pierre Elliott Trudeau, Janet Reno, Deborah Kerr, Alan Alda, and many others. But first I would like to take a few minutes to explain the difficulties that neurologists face when making a precise diagnosis of this disease, as demonstrated by the examples of Johnny Cash and Charles Schulz.

A number of Parkinson's symptoms may occur in other diseases or are a common part of the normal aging process. Take, for example, my Grandmother Gravel, who died at the venerable age of ninety-two. Her head shook at times, especially when she was playing cards, but to my knowledge, no one ever mentioned Parkinson's. Her tremors were simply due to old age, like wrinkles, white hair, and memory loss (which, however, never affected her during bridge).

There's no simple test for detecting this disease. To be certain that a patient has it, the doctor must open up the skull, remove the brain to examine the substantia nigra, then put it back in place. As yet, no volunteers have come forward. Neurologists make a diagnosis through observation and elimination, just as James Parkinson did over two centuries ago.

All the same, some diagnoses are indisputable. Both the preacher Billy Graham and Pope John Paul II definitely had Parkinson's. I don't plan to recruit either of them for my celestial team. I'll leave them to you. In any case, why would I need a pope if I'm already in heaven? If they want to sing the Lord's praises while I play cards with my grandmother, good for them.

# The Dictators' Disease

A NUMBER OF HISTORIANS CLAIM that Adolf Hitler had Parkinson's disease. Even though there's no conclusive proof, since no autopsy was performed, this hypothesis strikes me as quite likely. In fact, observers noted that his left hand, which he often hid behind his back, shook so badly that he went to great pains to control it. You can see these tremors in a number of videos on YouTube. Reliable witnesses also remarked that his gait appeared to be hesitant, and he had a stooped posture.

Several specialists claim, however, that these symptoms are associated with syphilis, an illness he had for a long time. It should also be noted that his personal physician, Theodor Morell, prescribed a ton of medications for him, in particular barbiturates, opioids, and cocaine.

Even if you take the Parkinson's hypothesis into consideration, you might doubt the pertinence of the following statement I found on Slate, a very popular website (I assume, since it's one of the first that appeared when I googled *Hitler and Parkinson's*). It's translated here from Leïla Marchand's July 1, 2015, article "La maladie de Parkinson a pu influencer les décisions d'Hitler," but I swear that I haven't invented a word of it:

> What effect does Parkinson's disease have as it slowly eats away at the brain of a strategist responsible for war crimes and crimes against humanity?... This is the question that a group of American neurobiologists set out to study. Their hypothesis was that Parkinson [sic] shaped the Führer's personality, so that he became more inhuman and more ruthless. Just as his paranoia increased his virulent antisemitism, his illness had an impact on a major part of his career and his decisions, causing him to become impulsive and rash, and, eventually, led to his losing the Second World War. Hitler was

known for his lack of remorse and sympathy, which can be associated with his illness.

When I end up in heaven along with my new friends, I won't miss the nonsense that can be found on the internet.

You might console yourself by considering the fact that other even more absurd explanations for Hitler's insanity can be found. It's often mentioned, for example, that he had only one testicle. Obviously, this malformation explains everything. When the young Hitler discovered his testicular deficiency, he decided, "In that case, I will seek revenge by starting a world war, and I will exterminate Jews, homosexuals, and Gypsies. And if I have some time left, I'll get rid of Africa too." All because of a missing testicle. If the physicians who noticed this anomaly had had the bright idea of transplanting an additional two dozen onto him, there would have been peace.

*  *  *

ACCORDING TO A NUMBER OF sources, Mao Zedong also had Parkinson's disease, though others mention syphilis, recurrent strokes (he smoked like a chimney and had poor personal hygiene), and, eventually, amyotrophic lateral sclerosis, a hypothesis to which most historians now subscribe. As a result, Parkinson's disease cannot be held responsible for either the Great Leap Forward or the Cultural Revolution. However, Mao appeared to have been testicularly normal, since he always kept several young proteges close at hand and treated them with great care, in every possible way. The last of these was Zhang Yufeng, whom he met when she (officially) turned eighteen. At the time, he was sixty-eight.

Stalin could not join our team: he died of a stroke, as did Salazar. Pol Pot? Weakened by malaria, he died of a heart attack. Idi Amin? Kidney failure.

Which leaves Franco, who received the following diagnosis: Parkinson's disease, coronary disease, recurrent acute peptic ulcer with frequent heavy bleeding, bacterial peritonitis, acute renal insufficiency, thrombophlebitis, bronchopneumonia, septic shock, and cardiac arrest. And that's not all. Ana Puigvert, a Spanish andrologist, told a reporter from the newspaper *El Mundo* that

Franco had only one testicle. She acquired this vital information from her grandfather, Antonio Puigvert, a renowned urologist who had Francisco Franco as a patient.

It must be true: I read it on the internet!

Ha!

# Melting Clocks

I'M WARY OF ANY NEWSPAPER article that starts with "According to a recent study."

If you do a Google search on those words, you'll get twenty million references in a fraction of a second, which is twice the number you'll get if you type in *tips for losing weight*. Just imagine our planet as a gigantic hive in which thousands of brains are abuzz, day and night, in the hopes of discovering something that will be written up by a reporter who won't have the time to read the study in question, which won't prevent them from announcing that, according to a recent study, simultaneously walking and chewing gum

encourages weight loss. Believe it or not, I heard
this vital information this very morning on the
airwaves of our national radio service.

Nonetheless, some studies are quite surprising. For example, in one published in the
journal *Neuropsychology*, you learn that a team of
researchers examined over two thousand paintings by two artists who had Parkinson's disease,
Salvador Dalí and Norval Morrisseau, and two
painters who had Alzheimer's disease, Willem de
Kooning and James Brooks. It seems the works by
the artists with Alzheimer's decreased in complexity starting when they were forty years old—in
other words, well before their illness was diagnosed. Paintings by Dalí and Morrisseau, on the
other hand, demonstrated an increase in the size
of the fractal dimension when the artists were
in midlife, followed by a decline as they neared
sixty. Dalí was diagnosed with Parkinson's disease
at age seventy-six, when his right hand began to
shake violently. As for Morrisseau, he was sixty-
five when he learned he had the disease.

Since any scientific research worth its salt
includes a control group, the researchers
compared these results with those for Chagall,

Monet, and Picasso, whose paintings showed increasing complexity over the years.

These observations seem to prove that Parkinson's and Alzheimer's diseases take root in the brain many years before the illnesses manifest themselves, leading to interesting prospects for future research.

According to a recent study, however, Dalí's habit of waxing his moustache with toad sperm has nothing to do with Parkinson's, any more than did his homage to Hitler, who, according to Dalí, had four testicles.

# Dark Thoughts

A FEW YEARS AGO, I PUBLISHED a short story collection titled *Idées noires*, which can be translated as "Dark Thoughts." One of these stories, "Une question d'équilibre" ("A Balancing Act"), starts like this: "I suppose that you can profoundly hate one of your parents and still live a balanced life, but surely it's easier to do so when you hate them both equally."

I'm still quite pleased with this opening, but not so thrilled with a sentence that appears a little later: "You might have described it as a Venus by Botticelli painted by a new-age artist with a mild case of Parkinson's, or a young girl in the flower of her youth photographed by a David Hamilton who put a little too much Vaseline on his camera lens."

It's not very funny. And anyway, who remembers that photographer, aside from a few pedophiles?

But it gets worse. In another short story in the same collection, I found this passage: "He stares at the screen, perplexed, and suddenly sees the number 4 appear on the 'Friend Requests' icon. It must be a mistake, he says to himself. It must be someone who is even less proficient than he is when it comes to new technology, if that's possible, or an old man who has Parkinson's disease and has tapped on the same key four times."

During the editing process, I must have reread these stories at least ten times without noticing the repetition in such a brief collection of the same tasteless image.

These stories were published two years before I received my diagnosis. Is it rational to think that my imagination *knew about it before I did*, so to speak? That my brain tried to warn me?

Everything may already have been said, but evidently fiction still has a future.

# Two Models

WHEN YOU HAVE AN INCURABLE disease, the attitude to adopt is not something you learn in elementary school, much less university, at least not if you're studying economics. In this area, as in so many others, you have to patch together something that corresponds as closely as possible to your personality using sketchy information gleaned here and there, at random. Our psychological models go back to early childhood, and it can take years to decode them.

As the fifth in a family of six children, I had the opportunity to learn a vast range of behaviours that were more or less adapted to this kind of situation.

My mother, who died when she was a hundred years old, never had a serious illness. If she had, we would have known about it. Oh, would we ever have known about it!

With my father, it was quite the opposite. Gérard belonged to that generation of men who, on occasion, would discuss politics, sports, or electronics, if called for, but never their illnesses, and even less their feelings. To get them to speak about their emotions, you would have had to torture them. Yet this man of few words would have had much to say on the subject of illness. Among other things, he suffered from diabetes for many years and had to bear the terrible consequences. When he turned sixty, he had a leg amputated and learned how to walk again, using a cane. A few years later, his other leg was removed, and once again he recovered, managing to walk a few steps with the help of two artificial limbs. But in the end, cancer got the better of him. He was never heard to utter a word of complaint.

I hope I haven't followed my mother's example. Self-pity is an unpleasant attitude, not to mention a complete waste of time. As a famous Albanian proverb states, there is no point in talking about your problems: 90 percent of people couldn't care less, and the remaining 10 percent will gloat over your misfortune (feel free to modify the ratios as you wish).

My father's attitude, while admirable in many ways, strikes me as exaggerated. Who would want to return to an era when men were required to wear armour? The ideal would be to complain a little—just enough. Illness has to serve some purpose, doesn't it? When I was little and was confined to my bed, didn't I deserve a bendy straw to make up for my woes?

So I don't think I'm being too unreasonable when I ask Michèle to help me chop the vegetables. I could handle it myself without too much difficulty—it's just a matter of taking the time—but I grab every opportunity to have her at my side. I'd be a fool not to take advantage of the situation.

If you knew her, you would do the same.

# Dreaming

HERE ARE A FEW OF the dreams I had this week:
I was the hero of a spy story told in the style of
Hergé and illustrated in Prismacolor, in which
Tintin himself makes a whirlwind appearance;
I taught an economics class which, for once, was
a success, about the negative effects of protec-
tionism; I remixed the album *Help* with Ringo
Starr in the Abbey Road studios; I wrote an absolutely idiotic screenplay for a crime movie, but
the female protagonist stole the show; I rode fifty
kilometres on my bike through the west end of
town and, along the way, saw an overpass collapse
due to an engineers' strike; I tried out characters

from children's books in a church; I was the hero in a Coen brothers' movie in which a life coach tried to recruit me by offering me a dream home and a calendar. I'll spare you my erotic dreams, shot in 3D, but I should mention that it's Tuesday and the week has just begun.

Ever since Colonel Parkinson enlisted me in his army, there's no end to these fascinating dreams, so much so that I'm considering cancelling my Netflix subscription and going to bed a little earlier each night to take advantage of them.

As strange as it may seem, there's a connection between Parkinson's and the production of dreams, or rather one's awareness of them. In fact, the phases of REM sleep, during which dreams are produced, appear to be longer in people who have Parkinson's. And since they wake during the night more often than normal sleepers, they recall their dreams more easily.

Unfortunately, the corollary is that they also remember their nightmares, which is not quite as pleasant.

Do people with Parkinson's have nightmares as often as other people? I don't know, but I do know that it's not uncommon for them to have harrowing nights. As for me, so far, I can't complain.

Sleep presents another surprising particularity for people with Parkinson's: at times, they may act out their dreams as if they're really experiencing them. The lock that paralyzes our muscles during the phases of REM sleep is located in the middle of the cerebral stem, in the lower part of the brain, where dopamine is produced—or no longer produced. Agitated sleep is often an early symptom of Parkinson's disease, and a number of couples choose to sleep in separate bedrooms, which strikes me as a wise decision.

Recently, I had an upsetting experience. No doubt dreaming that I was Muhammad Ali, I gave my pillow a serious thrashing. The punches I threw were so violent they woke me up. I don't dare think what might have happened had I attacked my wife that way. What if I dream one day that I'm Alfred Hitchcock showing his assistants how to film the shower scene? Or I go hunting for pterodactyls with my crossbow? Or a paranoid king puts me in charge of defenestration? Having a fertile imagination is not always such a good thing.

# Speaking

FOR 30 YEARS OR SO, my job involved speaking about economics to 150 students, divided into groups of 30. I won't go so far as to say that I always managed to hold their interest, especially on Monday mornings, but I can assure you that my voice carried right to the back of the classroom.

A little later, when my principal occupation was writing stories for children, I'd often find myself addressing hundreds of schoolchildren crammed into a gymnasium. I almost always refused to use the microphone that was provided.

I also frequently found myself in school libraries with groups of teenagers who went to great lengths to pretend they weren't listening to me. They were very successful at it, at least until they gave themselves away by laughing at one of my well-oiled jokes. I don't know whether they found the rest of my talk enthralling, but I'm positive they could hear me.

Today, these performances strike me as extraordinary accomplishments. If you think about it, speaking is *always* an accomplishment. It's a routine action that requires the participation of more than fifty muscles—the tongue alone has five, as has the larynx, not to mention the glottis, lips, intercostal muscles, and diaphragm. Not only do you have to produce sounds using all of this apparatus, you also have to *make sense*, and sense that is relevant to the person to whom you're speaking.

All of these muscles are controlled by dopamine. Since the brain is extremely adaptable, it still manages to do the job for someone with Parkinson's, but it requires them to perform a complex sort of gymnastics in order to produce and combine the thirty-six phonemes used in speaking French (forty-two for you English speakers). Now when I speak, I often feel like I've just come back from visiting a dentist who didn't skimp on the local anaesthetic.

The difficulty is not only muscular. Speech, like writing, demands a series of highly voluntary movements that require speed and precision. It's not in the least surprising that Parkinson's wreaks havoc with it.

Just as there is an area of the brain in charge of paralyzing you while you sleep to prevent you from acting out your karate dreams, there is also an area responsible for assessing the level of ambient sound and, accordingly, adjusting the volume of your voice. In someone with Parkinson's, this area is no longer functional, which makes conversation difficult, particularly in restaurants or any place where there is background noise. Even in an ideal environment, people often ask me to repeat what I've just said, which is extremely frustrating since I always feel like I've made a great effort to speak clearly.

Volume is not the only problem: over time the voice of someone who has Parkinson's grows hoarser and is at times shaky, the tone is monotonous, articulation is imprecise, and the pace is either too fast or too slow. In trying to conserve dopamine, a person with Parkinson's tends to provide fewer nonverbal clues, such as facial movements and expressions, making communication even more complicated. What's more, the disease can lead to a stuttering problem, or accentuate one that already exists. Which is the case for me, and I'm dismayed to find that I have new ways of stuttering, while the old tricks I've spent a lifetime perfecting no longer work.

It's a damn good thing I decided to become a writer.

# Writing

I LEARNED THIS TRICK FROM a friend who, in turn, learned it from another friend who has Parkinson's. Frustrated with the difficulty he was having in forming letters, he decided to buy some graph paper and write the way we used to in elementary school, slowly and using the lines as a guide.

I liked this idea. I went to my favourite stationery store, where I found something even better than graph paper: notebooks with lined paper, just like I had in grade one, with streets and sidewalks! Double-lined notebooks, we called them. I still remember Madame Boucher explaining to us that the letters *a* and *e* weren't allowed to go into the street, while *h* and *p* could. In those days, we didn't refer to ascenders and descenders, but rather heads and tails.

In the evening, while Michèle talks to her mother on the phone, I open my notebook, sharpen my HB pencils, put on some music, and align my vowels and consonants, which is easy enough, and then whole words, which is definitely more challenging. As strange as this may seem to someone who doesn't have Parkinson's, it requires great concentration to join the two edges of the sidewalks, and if the word has three syllables or more, it's nearly impossible. This results in *Canadian Confederations* and *progressive convolutions*, whatever that means. If I pause in the middle of a word, it becomes something like *erratic behaviour*. On the other hand, for "Lili's papa smokes his pipe," it's fine, though I still have to make an effort.

So that's where I am after sixty years of practising penmanship: two-syllable autonomy.

All the same, it's not an unpleasant endeavour. Memories waft to the surface as I do these exercises: I see little François, in grade one, struggling with his capital *F*s and *G*s; I think about my friend

Bernard, who always worked harder than I did and, as a result, was at the top of the class more often than I was (that's the sole reason, Bernard!); and finally, I recall poems I composed in ink and long handwritten letters that, as a teenager, I committed to paper at a time when word processing was still science fiction.

Since I don't have anything specific to write, I amuse myself by doing automatic writing exercises or picking up words as they float around the room: Hello, it's Michèle, no, no news from the twins, superfluous, oops, it's starting again, you need to concentrate, superfluous, superfluous, superfluous, you've almost got it, *let it be*, pal, *let it be*...

# Mysteries

FOR YEARS, I USED TO SING while making supper
or cleaning the house. No one ever suggested I cut
a record, but occasionally it happened, probably
quite by accident, that I managed to sing in key for
a measure or two. Now my singing is absolutely
disastrous. My kettle produces a more pleasant
sound. Since I have a smidgen of pride, I've quit
singing. Oddly, no one has complained.

Some people with Parkinson's don't have this
problem and sing so well they even join choirs.

For others, their gait is so hesitant, people
suspect they've had too much to drink. But when
they hop on a bike, they could pedal across Canada

without even touching the handlebars (while allowing for a few rest stops). In my case, I still walk holding myself relatively upright and go jogging every second day, for which my neurologist has congratulated me, but I've given up riding a bike because I'm afraid of losing my balance.

I've read testimonials from people with Parkinson's who claim that gardening does them a world of good. As for me, I completely freeze up the minute I get down on my knees and am faced with a clump of earth crawling with worms and earwigs. I suspect, in this instance, that the lack of dopamine stimulates bile and bad faith.

# No Connection

I SLEPT WELL LAST NIGHT. I didn't have any karate dreams, or else my pillow chose not to retaliate. I had a decent breakfast and drank my coffee (delicious) while doing my crossword puzzle (stimulating, just like my coffee). Then I went for my morning jog while thinking about a novel for teens that I'll get to work on as soon as this book is done. It will be set in the nineteenth century and will start off in an orphanage. My head is already teeming with characters. I can't wait to begin. Watch out, Dickens!

When I got home, I did my exercises, then tore down the vines that were choking the cherry trees. I thought about making jam before the birds destroyed the crop, but decided to wait until tomorrow.

I had just about an hour to write a few lines of the previous chapter of this book. I'd barely begun when it was already time for lunch. I enjoyed my meal, played a game of Scrabble with Michèle while sipping another cup of coffee, and had a nap.

In the afternoon, I treated myself to another hour of writing and then went to the post office on foot, less to see what was in the mail than for the pleasure of going for a walk.

When I got home, I made supper ("Would you cut the cucumber, please?") and we ate, played another game of Scrabble (Twice in one day? Absolutely! We like to indulge ourselves), and then, to end the evening, watched an episode of our favourite miniseries.

What's the connection with Parkinson's, you ask? There is none. Or rather, I just felt like pointing out that I'm also a normal human being, and a particularly fortunate one: when the creator put me together, he installed a lot of free games in my head—there's always something interesting going on in there. If I believed in him, I'd thank him.

# Freeze!

ONE OF THE MOST COMMON symptoms of Parkinson's is freezing (it's called that in French too: *le freezing*). I haven't yet experienced this frightening ordeal, but it's unlikely I'll escape it altogether. Some websites present it as a consequence of Parkinson's, while others say it's a side effect of the medication. A site I frequently consult states that these freezing episodes can happen "when your medication has the desired effect, when it doesn't have the desired effect, or in either case." Frankly, I don't see what other options there are.

Freezing can happen at any time, most often when the patient is walking or wants to start walking. You suddenly become a statue: your feet refuse to leave the ground, or else you trip, finding yourself unable to transfer your body weight from one leg to the other in order to move forward. The mere presence of an obstacle can trigger this reaction—a cluttered area, a doorway, the edge of a sidewalk—as can a large empty space, such as a parking lot. The result is that a person who has Parkinson's will remain frozen for several seconds, or even several minutes. You can imagine the problem this presents when it happens as you're about to get on an escalator, for example, or cross the street.

Some people with Parkinson's who have had this kind of experience react by leaving the house as little as possible. I understand that, but it would take a lot before I would resign myself to it.

When I think about eventually giving up my jogging session due to severe small-stepism (I run so slowly it's almost as if I'm walking in place), I plan to replace it with brisk walking, then slower and even slower walking, hoping to keep going until I'm ninety-eight years old. I would then take a two-week vacation, but no more than that.

In the meantime, I never leave the house

without making sure I have enough money on me
to pay for a taxi, just in case, and I'm extremely
careful when crossing the street. If I freeze, I can
try one of the suggestions offered on various
websites: breathe deeply, stand up straight and
look where I'm going, climb over a small imaginary
obstacle, count out loud, sing, think of Colonel
Parkinson chanting, "Left, right, left, right..." In
short, relearn how to walk. Step by step, day by
day, never taking anything for granted.

For a long time, I believed Parkinson's was a
disease. Now, I realize it's a philosophy course.

# The Chance of a Lifetime

WHEN MICHAEL J. FOX LEARNED he had Parkinson's disease, he wrote an autobiography titled *Lucky Man: A Memoir*. I don't know about you, but I have a hard time associating luck with Parkinson's. I understand that it's important to maintain a positive attitude, but there are limits. Any luckier than that, your name is Lou Gehrig and your doctor has just told you that you have an incurable disease, with only one or two years left to live.

Shortly after he was forced to retire, that same Lou Gehrig delivered a memorable speech to fans gathered in a stadium packed to the rafters—an achievement even more impressive because he suffered from stage fright at the mere thought of speaking before an audience. After all, his job was hitting balls, which he did at a speed as impressive as Babe Ruth's.

I'll take the liberty here of reproducing a few excerpts from his now famous speech, as quoted in "Luckiest Man" on the National Baseball Hall of Fame website:

> For the past two weeks you have been reading about a bad break. Yet today I consider myself the luckiest man on the face of the earth. I have been in ballparks for seventeen years and have never received anything but kindness and encouragement from you fans....
>
> When the New York Giants, a team you would give your right arm to beat, and vice versa, sends you a gift—that's something. When everybody down to the groundskeepers and those boys in white coats remember you with trophies—that's something. When you have a wonderful mother-in-law who takes sides with you in squabbles with her own daughter—that's something. When you have a father and a mother who work all their lives so

you can have an education and build your body—it's a blessing. When you have a wife who has been a tower of strength and shown more courage than you dreamed existed—that's the finest I know.

So I close in saying that I might have been given a bad break, but I've got an awful lot to live for.

I'm touched by this speech every time I read it. Come to think of it, Lou Gehrig and Michael J. Fox were both extremely lucky to have reached the pinnacle of their respective careers, and their illness allowed them to appreciate their luck. This attitude makes me think of the reaction we all have when dealing with a brief ailment, be it an abscessed tooth or a massive cold. You dream of the moment when you'll feel better and promise yourself to thoroughly enjoy it, but as soon as you do feel better, you forget your promise and go about your daily life without giving good health another thought.

When you have a degenerative disease, you know for certain you'll never recover. So you tell yourself to enjoy how you're feeling today, because it could be worse tomorrow.

# A Few Remedies

LIKE A NUMBER OF PHYSICIANS of his time, James Parkinson prescribed purges and good old-fashioned bloodletting at the base of the neck. A person with Parkinson's who lived in India five thousand years earlier would have had better luck: Indian traditional medicine described several movement disorders that resembled Parkinson's, and as treatment, recommended eating *Mucuna pruriens*, popularly called velvet bean, a variety of snow pea that's a pretty purple colour. We had to wait five millennia to learn that the inner part of the pod of this plant contains levodopa, the remedy used today.

Charcot, on the other hand, never missed an

opportunity to mention that belladonna alka-
loids should be "the daily bread of the Parkinson's
patient," as he did in his *Leçons cliniques sur les
maladies des vieillards et les maladies chroniques*.
Before going to purchase belladonna from your
favourite witch (it's in the same section as the
mandrake, near the powdered snake spit), I suggest
you research its side effects. Personally, I prefer
that Michèle call me "my mover and shaker" rather
than "my late husband."

Since we are in the plant department, you will
certainly be delighted to learn that homeopaths
sell large quantities of pills that are purported to
help those with Parkinson's. For example, I read
on the internet that swallowing gelsemium pills
three times a day can simultaneously cure both
ocular migraine and emotional diarrhea. Feel free
to trust them, but I would be wary of anyone who
recommends taking glucose and platinum pills
to cure lesbianism. I'm quite serious. *Glucose.* In
*homeopathic* doses. To *cure* lesbianism. I'm all for
having an open mind, but I don't like to be taken
for an idiot.

In fact, the only therapy that manages to
relieve some Parkinson's symptoms, as levodopa

does, and delays their onset, is physical exercise. Walking is highly recommended, as are boxing, dance, and tai chi. I prefer to indulge in jogging, a matter of habit, and see a kinesiologist who has designed an exercise program for me with the aim of improving my posture, agility, and balance. I also consulted a speech therapist, who suggested intensive therapy sessions to improve my speaking, and which I found very effective. In short, I spend a decent part of my day exercising. I don't know if it's as good as they say for delaying the onset of certain symptoms of Parkinson's, but it keeps me busy and is excellent for morale.

Michael J. Fox suggests devoting oneself to meditation to reduce tremors. Why not? However, one shouldn't feel obliged to study transcendental meditation with the notorious Maharishi Mahesh Yogi or one of his disciples (who, sadly, are legion): mindfulness meditation, devoid of any religious hocus-pocus, will do just as well.

There are several kinds of meditation, with various names: sitting, standing, walking, short, long, lake, mountain, breathing…I enjoy practising all of them, but my favourite is the one I do every day after lunch, which I call snoring meditation.

The idea, as you will have gathered, is to do something that makes you feel good.

* * *

THE ONLY EFFECTIVE REMEDY FOR Parkinson's is levodopa, a substance whose effects weren't really understood until the 1960s. When the body receives its dose, it transforms levodopa into dopamine. As it's precisely the absence of dopamine that causes the disease, you might assume that's all there is to it. But if it were that simple, Parkinson's would be eradicated from the planet. We wouldn't talk about it any more than we discuss the plague, smallpox, or polio, and I would have something else to do instead of writing this book.

The first problem facing researchers was that most of the levodopa taken orally was transformed into dopamine before it reached the brain. So large doses were administered that produced only modest, short-lived results, with major side effects. (I hate to imagine how many velvet beans one would have to ingest to obtain a similar result.)

A substance known as a decarboxylase inhibitor was then discovered. It prevents dopamine from being wasted, and all currently prescribed medications containing levodopa also include an inhibitor that allows the dopamine to cross the blood-brain barrier and reach the brain.

While levodopa significantly reduces Parkinson's symptoms, it doesn't cure the disease. The neurons in the substantia nigra cannot be miraculously resuscitated, and they continue to die off, making it necessary to constantly adjust the dosage of the medication.

Other medications can reduce some symptoms, but at times they produce strange side effects. For example, some patients have difficulty resisting urges, whether related to pathological gambling, compulsive shopping, or hypersexuality. I leave it to you to imagine the resulting problems for some couples.

A surgical intervention called deep brain stimulation, which involves implanting electrodes in the brain and linking them to a stimulator placed under the skin, has apparently had good results, but for the time being, it is reserved for patients who are at an advanced phase of the illness and for whom all other treatments have failed. I'm not there yet. Far from it.

As I write this, I've just celebrated my sixty-seventh birthday and have barely started taking levodopa. I hope to benefit from its positive effects for twelve or thirteen years, at which point I would be exactly eighty years old. By then, I will officially be old, and no one will be taken aback by my odd movements.

# Honeymoon

I IMAGINE THAT ONE OF the worst things about being a neurologist must be delivering a diagnosis of Parkinson's, Alzheimer's, multiple sclerosis, or epilepsy to a patient. On the other hand, prescribing levodopa to someone with Parkinson's disease must be one of their favourite activities: the patient is promised nothing less than a honeymoon. This is no exaggeration: most patients experience considerable relief from their symptoms, with minimal side effects, for a few years—you will agree, this is a remarkable length of time for a honeymoon to last. Levodopa will continue to work during the subsequent years, though it won't be as effective.

Two years after my official induction into the Parkinson's club, I am just starting to take these little pills, and I can attest to their effectiveness. One hour after I swallow the first pill, a series of amazing little miracles occurs. Once the pill is absorbed by the small intestine, the chemical molecules make their way to the brain through the bloodstream and take over from the substantia nigra to produce brand-new dopamine, which then rushes to transmit the good news to the muscles via the nervous system: "Hey guys, I'm back! What are you waiting around for? Now's the time to write in cursive letters, double-click your mouse, slice bread, grate cheese, play the cup-and-ball game, and button your cassock." I can even take my wallet out of my back pocket and put it back without difficulty. It may not seem like a big deal, but it's most enjoyable, believe me.

Okay, obviously levodopa is not perfect. I have a constant feeling of fatigue, but I'm no longer twenty years old, and not everything is due to Parkinson's. I'm not as stiff as I was, though I'm not planning to sign up for a Frisbee tournament or an embroidery class anytime soon. There's a good chance that I'd be beaten in a pistol duel, so for the next little while I'll steer clear of the Wild West.

My neurologist is not making any promises, but I gather that this grace period could last ten years, and perhaps even a little longer, especially if I continue to stay in shape. Which is a good thing: I still have so many stories to tell.

# Go for It, Researchers! Go, Go, Go!

JUDGING FROM THE TALK SHOWS and the magazines I see at my dentist's office, my contemporaries are primarily interested in ear-splitting songstresses, European princesses, appallingly predictable comedians, photogenic chefs, and certain starlets who've become famous by virtue of their cleavage and who continue to be famous because they're famous.

It's not beneath me to turn my attention to their plight from time to time, which explains why I always arrive early at the dentist's. But the older I get, the more interested I am in scientists. For a while now, I've had a soft spot for those seeking a cure for Parkinson's disease. Go figure!

As there aren't any magazines in which to admire photographs of celebrity scientists emerging from their swimming pools, one has to imagine them in their white coats, wearing protective goggles and delicately manipulating burettes and pipettes in search of a miraculous cure.

My heroes are no longer named Maurice Richard and Victor Hugo, but Jungwoo, Wei, Caroline, Stefano, Abid, and Ariel, and they exist in a universe where there's no room for discrimination; these researchers may be any gender, race, religion, or ethnicity—no one gives a damn, as long as they're using their brains to find solutions for real problems. They come from the four corners of the earth, but they all speak the same language, that of science.

It's entirely possible that a researcher working alone in a village in Myanmar could, by chance, find a miraculous root (go, go, Myanmar!), but it's more likely that a discovery will come to light in a university lab. Looking at the list of subsidized research projects that deal with Parkinson's, it appears that micro-organisms found in the intestine can travel along the nerves and end up destroying the neurons in the notorious substantia nigra. If we could eliminate these micro-organisms before they get to the brain or convince them to do something that's more useful (tackle wrinkles or body fat, for example, which would certainly multiply research budgets by thousands), we could not only find effective medicines for relieving symptoms, but finally beat the disease.

The use of stem cells also leads to interesting prospects. These cells, as you may know, are reminiscent of Woody Allen's Leonard Zelig: they have zero personality. Inject them into the rear end of a television-watching couch potato and voilà—they turn into adipose tissue. Obviously, they could be put to better use: installed in the brain, stem cells would become brand-new black neurons and would produce dopamine. It's certainly easier to write about the treatment than to perform it, but it appears that Japanese researchers have successfully treated monkeys and are preparing to do clinical trials on humans. Go, Japan, go!

Other scientists are more interested in the role of mitochondria, enzymes, proteins, tomography, and lots of things that strike me as fascinating but are way beyond my scope. Allow me, however, to mention that some researchers are looking into transcranial magnetic stimulation, which thrills me. In 1985, I published a novel, *Bonheur fou*, (*Felicity's Fool*, in English), in which the action takes place a century earlier, with one of the main characters, Dr. Bernard Dansereau, using precisely this method when treating his patients at Hôpital St-Jean-de-Dieu. If the current research delivers promising results, I will gladly renounce all royalties from my invention.

Far be it from me to meddle in their affairs, but I would suggest that scientists study the molecules present in ice cream. I'm convinced they produce masses of top-quality dopamine.

In any event, I give scientists ten years to find a cure. Even if they don't succeed, I'll still be grateful for their efforts.

\* \* \*

THEIR NAMES ARE DORELLE, ALEXANDRA, Stéphanie, and Chan. They are Ph.D. students in neuroscience at the Université de Montréal and at McGill University, and they need people who have Parkinson's disease to be guinea pigs when testing various theories. Since I can't very well spend

entire days writing stories and doing diction exercises, I happily agreed to volunteer some of my
time. After all, it's in my interest and allows me
to spend time with individuals who are far more
stimulating than the people invited to appear on
the television talk shows.

Each time I meet with these researchers, they
ask me very difficult questions, such as "What
day is it today?" or "What do a banana and an
orange have in common?" and they congratulate me when I provide the right answer, which
is always a pleasure. They also ask me to draw a
clock and place the hands so that they indicate
ten past eleven, to draw a cube, or to differentiate a camel from a rhinoceros. After successfully
passing this test, Donald Trump declared before
a group of dumbfounded reporters that he was a
"very stable genius."

At each visit, the researchers ask me to touch
my nose with my index finger, an activity for
which I am the undisputed champion. I can even
do it ten times in a row! Having verified that
I too am a very stable genius, as well as a high-
level athlete, they put motion sensors on me and
ask me to perform certain activities—stand up,

sit down, walk on treadmills that move at various speeds, that sort of thing.

After all that, the last test is an MRI. Strapped in, my head immobilized, I feel like I'm a pencil about to be sharpened. Once I'm installed inside this diabolical machine, my job is to not move, which is quite easy, and to not think about anything for twenty minutes, which is another kettle of fish.

It's impossible to keep myself from thinking that one day I will be stretched out horizontally for a very long time, and I will succeed, then, in thinking about nothing. Absolutely nothing at all.

Does one really need to train for that?

## Beginning at the End

PLEASE FORGIVE THE SPOILER, BUT truth be told, in the end we all die. Yes, really.

You'll tell me that's one of life's certainties, like taxes, but a person who's aware that they have a degenerative disease views this inevitability differently. The Grim Reaper becomes more present, and in my case even more so because I received my diagnosis the same year the government sent me my first Old Age Security cheque, a reminder I receive every month, like clockwork. Like those clocks that keep ticking in the parlour, reminding the old folks, over and over again, "I'm waiting for you," as Jacques Brel sang in "Les Vieux."

Even if it's not fatal, Parkinson's disease puts you at risk for a number of things. A person with Parkinson's must try to avoid falling, for example, and needs to get used to having something to drink close at hand while they're eating; there are numerous instances of people who've choked. A weakened body can also harbour a lung infection. But Parkinson's doesn't in any way affect the life expectancy of those who have the disease, and they end up dying of stroke, cancer of the colon, or old age, just like everyone else. Their problem is not so much the certainty that they will die— something they share with other mortals—but knowing what shape they'll be in when they're summoned to that meeting. "Dying is no big deal," said Brel. "But getting old..."

Like all of us, my experience of death is very limited. In practice, it's zero. As for the theory, it's not much better. When I was a child, it was the priests' job to educate us about this subject. Some were very imaginative when describing the torments of hell, but were much less so when it came time to tell us about the joys of heaven. Spending eternity on a cloud singing the Lord's praises while playing the harp was not the most exciting of prospects; you mean to entice us by promising an uninterrupted series of boring Sundays? Really? Sitting at the right hand of God wasn't all that appealing, especially since it seemed impossible to sit at the right hand of a being who was everywhere.

If I'd been promised seventy-two virgins when I was a teenager, I might not have lost my faith quite so early. Though doubtless I would have wondered if those young girls could imagine themselves being offered seventy-two male virgins, which would have presented a serious logistical problem.

What's even worse is that we were promised the resurrection of the body at the end of time. The resurrection of the body? My God! To what purpose? Couldn't we finally become pure spirits? Unless I'm mistaken, this idea is still part of the credo. I would happily be resuscitated (after all, why not?), but would I be given my old man's body or that of my youth? And while we're at it, can I ask for a few cosmetic touch-ups? What about my friends, my parents, my exes—would they also be resuscitated? If so, how old would they be?

We never actually formulate these questions, doubtless suspecting that the answers we'd receive would be even more confusing. Also, perhaps we've already understood that it's better not to question people who claim to hold the truth.

Fortunately, early on in my life I encountered a mentor who taught me other ways of thinking about this topic. This wise man was Georges Brassens, the French singer-songwriter and poet. It's been a long while since I kept up to date on what's happening in popular music (has anything happened since the Beatles broke up?), but I doubt he's been replaced by anyone. Thanks to him I discovered the great pleasure to be found in visiting cemeteries and have always preferred funeral homes to nightclubs.

Perhaps also thanks to Brassens, at a very young age I came to terms with the idea of death and learned not to fear it unduly. The way I see it, I die each night when I fall asleep: I'm no longer aware of what's happening around me, and it's possible that I won't wake up.

And then? And then nothing. The universe was deprived of my presence for millions of years, and that didn't prevent it from growing and expanding. And if I'm already dead when it fizzles out? Too bad for the universe. My only regret is that

I won't be there to read all the articles that will be written on the subject.

One of my favourite songs by Brassens has always been "Le testament." While the whole song would be worth quoting, I'll start with the introduction, translated here by Tom Thomson, in which one encounters a mocking God who recycles the most hackneyed joke:

> I'll be sad like a weeping willow
> when the God who follows me everywhere
> says to me, his hand on my shoulder:
> "Off you go, up there to see if I'm there."

Not to mention this delightful quatrain:

> If it's necessary to go to the cemetery
> I will take the longest path,
> I'll play truant to the grave,
> I'll quit life reluctantly...

And this, a little bit later:

> I want to part for the other world
> by the scenic route.

Allow me to compile a short list of things I will leave behind without any hard feelings when my time is up: backaches, head colds, heat waves, blaring advertisements, neckties, singers screaming at the top of their lungs while I'm grocery shopping, plastic bags, mosquitos, show-offs in their convertibles, show-offs on their motorcycles, men's magazines, homeopaths, traffic jams, musical comedies, columnists with their ready-made ideas, those know-it-alls who are always right, pop singers who think they have the authority to make a declaration regarding the fate of the nation because they've composed a song that was a hit, root canals, the remorse I still feel regarding stupid things I did a half-century ago, shoelaces that break, bicycle chains that fall off, impatient honkers, pebbles in shoes, shopping centres, disco music, airports, procedures, organizational charts, high school cafeterias, mariachi singers who play at my table, trolls, general assemblies, cold soup, recorded messages that assure me my call is important, elevator music, bedbugs, technocrats, clauses in fine print, jellyfish, leeches, opera…

And Parkinson's? I would let it go as well, without any hard feelings. But with just a little regret, all the same.

# Postscript

I STILL HAVE A COUPLE of words for you, Colonel
Parkinson. You entered my brain on the sly, you
set up camp there without asking for permission,
and you slowly plundered my supply of black
cells—so slowly that it took years before I noticed
they were missing. Admit it, you snuck up on me
when I was off guard. One expects more courage
from a military man.

You caught me off guard, but I acknowledged
your victory without much complaint. I didn't
lash out, I didn't get plastered, I didn't take my
revenge on the entire universe or, notably, on
those closest to me. I swallowed my pill, literally

and figuratively, in the singular and in the plural. I consulted physicians, a kinesiologist, a psychologist, and a speech therapist. I continued to walk, run, read, and write. More and more slowly, undoubtedly, but all in all, I adapted rather well. Thanks to this experience, I even produced a book that I'm not unhappy with.

It's been a few years now since this book was first published in French. Obviously, since that time there hasn't been a cure. But I've discovered a miracle remedy: writing! It may not be a cure, but it seems to help forestall the inevitable decline and, one way or another, it feels good to air one's problems.

Since then, Colonel, not only have you not broken camp, but you've become quite comfortable, settling in and making yourself feel at home, to such a degree that it's impossible to forget your presence for an hour, let alone for a day.

Three years later, the symptoms I describe in this book are still present, a little more severe at times, or more visible. The tremors start earlier in the day, and it would now be difficult to read a book if I held it in my right hand. Fortunately, there are electronic tablets.

I still have trouble taking my wallet out of my back pocket, and it's not just because I'm stingy. My right foot is often stiff, and I have to talk to it to convince it to relax, which, fortunately, it willingly accepts. If this last sentence strikes you as strange, that's because you don't have Parkinson's; in fact, almost all kinds of movement are possible, provided you send different commands and use other circuits in the brain. However, this doesn't always work. No matter how hard I try, I haven't found a way to wink, which deprives me of a weapon of mass seduction, something which, fortunately for all, I have never abused. Swallowing also poses a few problems. When I want to speak, first I have to *think* about swallowing my saliva, in addition to engaging in the usual vocal gymnastics. This interferes with spontaneity, to say the least. It can also happen that my arm, even when it's immobile, shakes on the inside—there again, those with Parkinson's will understand me. If I don't pay attention to my posture, I feel at times like I've stepped into Joe Cocker's skin when he was singing "With a Little Help from My Friends" at Woodstock.

But you already know all of this, don't you, Colonel?

Now I have a favour to ask of you. I'd like you to avert your eyes for a few moments. I would like to talk about stylistics with my readers, and I'm afraid you'll be bored. That's right, stylistics. It's not the sort of subject that fascinates colonels. In the meantime, could you engage in some normal military activities? Peel some potatoes, for example, or polish your boots, or intimidate recruits by yelling insults two inches in front of their faces. I promise, I need only a few moments. Two or three pages, at most. That's it.

\* \* \*

ARE YOU STILL THERE, DEAR reader? Let's keep our voices down while the colonel buffs his boots. Perfectionist that he is, the old coot will be kept busy for a while. By now, I'm starting to know his weak points.

First, I want to thank you for keeping me company all this time. I take your presence as silent proof of your friendship, and I assure you that it's precious.

Let's reflect on stylistics. If you're a professor of literature, a professional copy editor, or simply an attentive reader, you may have noticed that I've committed a serious crime in this postscript, and in the rest of the book, by indulging in annoying repetitions of two words. What makes the crime even more serious is that those two words are adverbs. Hemingway advised avoiding them at all costs.

You know what? I don't care what Hemingway said. What matters to me is that there might be some people among my readers who have just learned that they have this disease and who are still Parkinstunned. They will undoubtedly forgive me for not setting off on a futile search for synonyms. I would like them to know that I deliberately increased the occurrence of the words *slowly* and *fortunately*, which seem to me to be of equal importance.

I'm no physician, but all those I've consulted have repeated that while this disease develops differently in each individual, it progresses *slowly*, very *slowly*. One has time to see it coming, to get used to it, to react, to adapt. And when it comes to reacting, nothing beats exercise. Many studies, in fact, show that it's the only effective method for slowing the progression of the disease. Even if that weren't so, exercise is good for one's morale.

You don't need to run a marathon or break records in the hundred-metre hurdles. In any case, the colonel would catch up with you pretty quickly if you tried. It's better to fool him by being slower than he is; that way, he's more likely to forget about you.

Many very enjoyable activities are notable for their slowness: meditation, tai chi, yoga, Scrabble, listening to music, reading, writing...You might even indulge in certain exercises that Leonard Cohen alluded to in "Slow," one of his last songs. In the first verse, he points out that going fast just isn't his thing, that he doesn't mind getting there last, not due to his being old but just because he's always preferred to take it slow.

The second adverb I abused is *fortunately*. As in: Fortunately, there are other things to do in life aside from playing Frisbee. Fortunately, slowness can be cultivated. Fortunately, there are computers, electronic tablets, and electric toothbrushes. Fortunately, levocarb, rasagiline, Lax-A-Day, and naproxen all exist. And most of all, fortunately, there are doctors, researchers, pharmacists, speech therapists, physiotherapists, support groups, caring spouses, friends, children, and grandchildren...

Fortunately, there's the colonel, you say? I know that at times one needs to turn the other cheek and such, but let's not get carried away. Colonel Parkinson exists, and one has to put up with him, but no one should feel obligated to like him.

The old coot is stubborn, unpleasant, and intolerant, and he never backs down. But there's also life, all around us, which just keeps going on its merry way.

# Acknowledgements

IN WRITING THIS ACCOUNT, I SURFED the internet extensively. As usual, I found a lot of nonsense,
but also a great deal of interesting information.
Since I'm neither a doctor nor a historian, I hope I've
selected wisely from among the available sources.
The Parkinson Québec site was particularly helpful.

My thanks to doctors Jacques Rivest, Allan
Ryder-Cook, and Sylvain Chouinard, who guided
me as I learned about this disease.

Thanks to Ginette Mayrand, who has been a
precious source of information and encourage-
ment, and to Alice Mostlova, who helped me
regain my voice.

Thanks to Marie-Noëlle Gagnon, Danielle Laurin, the entire team at Québec Amérique, as well as to translator Shelley Pomerance and the team at House of Anansi Press.

Thanks to Michèle, as always and forever.

And finally, thanks to my brother Charles, a tireless detector of typographical errors, but not only that.

FRANÇOIS GRAVEL studied economics and taught at the Cégep level until 2006. He is the author of over a hundred books for children and adults, many of which have received awards and distinctions. His adult novels include *Ostende* and *Adieu, Betty Crocker*, which have both been translated into English. *Adieu, Betty Crocker* was a competing title in the 2014 edition of *Le combat des livres*, the French-language equivalent of *Canada Reads*. He splits his time between Montreal and Île-aux-Grues.

SHELLEY POMERANCE is the host of *Writers Unbound* on MAtv. For many years she was a presence on CBC Radio as an arts journalist and host. As a translator, Shelley has worked for the Power Plant Contemporary Art Gallery, the Montreal Museum of Fine Arts/Musée d'Orsay, Blue Metropolis Literary Festival, and many other cultural and civil society organizations. She lives in Montreal.